ACKNOWLEDGMENTS

I would like to acknowledge and give thanks to God who gave me this idea to spread technology to children and who always teaches me to step out on faith in accordance with His word. I would like to acknowledge my husband for being a great provider and supporter. I would like to acknowledge my mom for pushing me so that the greatness inside of me comes out and for always encouraging and supporting me. I would love to acknowledge and thank my 2 beautiful children who always has to be patient while I'm writing, designing and coding but they are my number one reason I push to leave a great legacy.

DEDICATION

This book is dedicated to all of the at home moms that endeavor to give their families all the love, support and best they have to offer.

A NOTE TO PARENTS

Thank you for your interest in the #CodePlayground series. By the end of this three part series, we would have created a web page that says, "Hello World My Name is [child's name]". Your young one will develop this page utilizing our fun and colorful books. There are three different books that are relevant to each blog in our three part series. Each book will focus on the three different parts of an HTML page; the document declaration <html>, the head section <head> and the body <body>.

So today's #CODEplayground activity is to learn about the first tag of an HTML document, called which is the document declaration, the <html> tag.

There is an associated blog located on CEO Mom Magazine. You can view the contents of this blog at the back of this book where the character building activity is **self-esteem**.

All volumes in this entire series are available on Amazon or can be purchased at http://codeplaygroundmovement.com

#CODEPLAYGROUND

SELF-ESTEEM ON THE PLAYGROUND

VOLUME I

WELCOME! LET'S PLAY ON THE PLAYGROUND

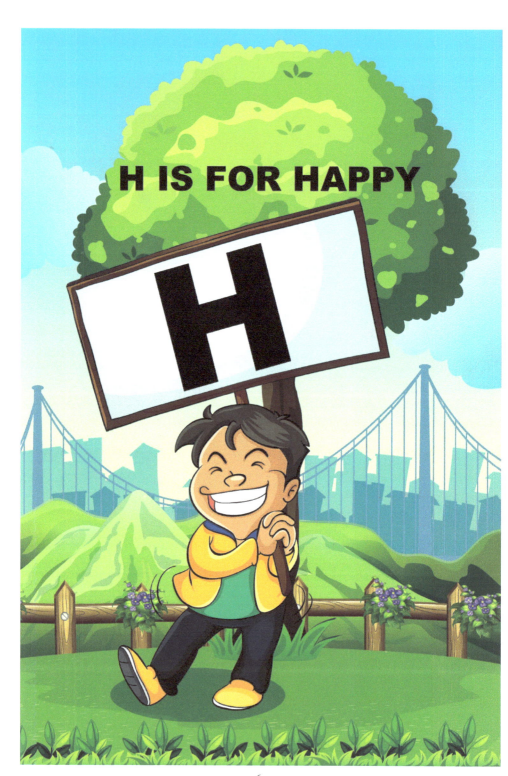

At the Playground
all of the kids are

HAPPY

T IS FOR TREE

They play under the

and enjoy the cherries.

M IS FOR
MERRY GO ROUND

The Merry children
take a spin on the

MERRY
GO
ROUND

L IS FOR LEAP
LOOK AT ME

At the Playground
all of the kids
LEAP for joy.

WHAT DOES THAT SPELL?

Now let's add the
Open Sign <

<HTML

Now let's add the Closed Sign >

HTML>

LET'S DO IT AGAIN

Let's add the Open Sign **<** *Again*

<HTML

Now let's add the Closed Sign but this time we end /> the tag with a /

HTML/>

YAY. WE WROTE OUR FIRST TAG CALLED HTML.

SEE YOU

NEXT TIME!

THE END

STEM...MOTHERHOOD...PROGRAMMING

As an at home "Mompreneur" with 2 toddlers, there are many challenges I face in the day-to-day life of work and play. I am constantly trying to come up with ideas that will allow me to stimulate my children and give them activities that we can learn from as well as do together. One of my biggest enjoyments is being able to be at home and see my children grow.

This is how #CODEplayground came about. #CODEPlayground is a delightful place where young and adult minds meet. Its goal is to stimulate the hearts and minds of children with hopes of stirring up their technical imagination. #CODEplayground is a place whee our children can see the world through the eyes of technology.

Purpose

As parents, we know how important it is to constantly stimulate and develop the character of our children. Our participation in our children's lives brings forth confidence. When it comes to balance, moms often find themselves consumed with life's everyday routines. It becomes more and more challenging to concentrate on our children's development as much as we would like.

There are several activities in our daily lives that we can do to promote the growth and stimulation of our children socially, educationally, morally and financially. When we participate in such activities, we allow them to learn how to explore themselves and find what gifting innately resides in them because of the training they have received from an early age.

Our hope is that this 3 part blog series induces awareness introducing activities that are FUN. We endeavor to help parents maximize the time they spend time with their children while building a community of young stars interested in

Our activities aim to build a children's self esteem, self perspective and self confidence.

Self Esteem Building

In Part I of this 3 Part series we will focus on self-esteem. The next two will focus on self-confidence and self-perspective respectively. According to Child Development Academy, self-esteem is a major key to success in a child's life. Their blog entry, Child Psychology and Mental Health, stresses the importance of having a great perception of one self because it promotes a happy and healthy life in children. This particular blog emphasizes the importance of parents doing activities with their kids that are not only intentional but specific in process and execution. These activities should be one-on-one if there are multiple children in the home as well as group activities for all the children that are in the home.

#CODEplayground not only assists in this objective but also induces an interest in programming from an early age. This adds to the arsenal of positive parental experiences that is so necessary for your child to have great self-esteem and it's also an experience your child will be able to remember and connect to when programming is introduced in their education.

#CODEplayground Activity

By the end of this three part series, we will have created a web page that says, "Hello World My Name is [child's name]". Your child will develop this page utilizing our fun and colorful books. There are three different books that are relevant to each blog in our three part series. Each book will focus on the three different parts of a HTML page. The document declaration <html>, the head section <head> and the body <body>

So today's #CODEplayground – Mommy, Me & Programming activity is to learn about the start of an HTML document.

Have fun programming with your child and building their self-esteem. Don't forget to give affirmations to your child as they go through the book.

You can view this blog on CEO Mom Magazine at the following link:
http://ceomommagazine.com/stemmotherhoodprogramming

ABOUT THE AUTHOR

Nikki Garcia is a Florida A&M University graduate in Computer Information Systems. She has been a developer for over 12 years. She worked for Keiser University for 9 years where she focused on lead generation and other webmaster tasks. She also worked for Safari Ltd. as a webmaster and a sleuth of freelancing jobs. She is the President of Personality Web Designs, Inc., which has successfully been in business since 2004 and Vice President of Resolute Solutions of the Palm Beaches. She is a work at home mom who has a passion for working with youth and developing their desire for technology. She has taught computers to the elderly through the City of Miami's Miami Elevate program in which she was featured in the Miami Herald for her outstanding work. She currently is one of the Success Coaches for the Billy Thompson Foundation in which she and her husband teach the Technology Academy, teaching youth about programming, robotics, and building computers.

Like us on FB: personalitywebdesign, Twitter: PersonalityWeb or visit our website at: http://www.personalityweb.com

www.ingramcontent.com/pod-product-compliance
Lightning Source LLC
LaVergne TN
LVHW012316070326
832902LV00001BA/27